Would You Believe...

the losers were killed in Mayan football?

and other **perilous** pastimes

Richard Platt

OXFORD
UNIVERSITY PRESS

Contents

OXFORD
UNIVERSITY PRESS

Great Clarendon Street, Oxford OX2 6DP

Oxford University Press is a department of the University of Oxford. It furthers the University's objective of excellence in research, scholarship, and education by publishing worldwide in

Oxford   New York

Auckland   Cape Town   Dar es Salaam   Hong Kong
Karachi   Kuala Lumpur   Madrid   Melbourne
Mexico City   Nairobi   New Delhi   Shanghai
Taipei   Toronto

With offices in

Argentina   Austria   Brazil   Chile   Czech Republic
France   Greece   Guatemala   Hungary   Italy   Japan
Poland   Portugal   Singapore   South Korea   Switzerland
Thailand   Turkey   Ukraine   Vietnam

Oxford is a registered trade mark of Oxford University Press in the UK and in certain other countries

Text copyright © Oxford University Press 2007

The moral rights of the author have been asserted

Database right Oxford University Press (maker)

First published 2007

British Library Cataloguing in Publication Data

Data available

ISBN-13: 978-0-19-911500-6

1 3 5 7 9 10 8 6 4 2

Originated by Oxford University Press

Created by BOOKWORK Ltd

Printed in China by Imago

WARNING: *The activities in this book are for information only and should not be tried at home!*

Introduction

WHAT DO YOU DO FOR FUN and to relax? Perhaps you play a computer game or read a book. Maybe you watch TV or kick around a ball with some friends. Have you ever thought about trying something a little different? How about going along to watch a couple of slaves fight to the death, or dressing in a tin suit and hurtling along on horseback in a mock battle?

These pastimes from the past seem weird now, but centuries ago they were respectable ways of spending idle afternoons. To stave off boredom, people also tried flying through the air like birds, or sliding down slopes on ice blocks. Today, we have improved on some of these ancient amusements – and thought of other equally strange or dangerous games.

Extreme sports, for instance, take your favourite sport and double the danger. Difficult, or downright deadly, wild games like BASE jumping or speed skiing push at the boundaries of what is possible – and legal. Other new games, like ostrich or pig racing, are safe enough but harmlessly mad. In the pages that follow you can read about all these peculiar pastimes, and learn how they grew to be popular.

Would You Believe...?

What, where, why, who?
What was the medieval punishment for hunting in royal forests? Where is there an annual bog-snorkelling race? Why did the spectators run from the Mayan ball-game stadium every time there was a goal? Who invented hang-gliders? If you want to find out the answers – read on!

Ancient Pastimes

Prehistoric games ▶
Carved from wood or shaped from clay, animal figures have always delighted small children. This timber tiger is from a tomb in Thebes, on the River Nile. An Egyptian child played with it some 3,500 years ago. It may have lost a leg, but its glinting glass eye and string-operated opening jaw give the beast an authentic snarl.

PEOPLE FROM THE DISTANT PAST had little time for play. Most children worked: they could scare birds from growing crops before they were even old enough to speak. When children had time to relax, their toys were simple and similar to the things with which smaller children grow up today – balls, dolls, animals and wheeled toys.

Would You Believe...?

Aztec wheels
The Aztec people of ancient Mexico made wheeled toys for children, but never used wheeled transport. Some experts suggest this was because carts and carriages were useless without animals to pull them: there were no horses in Mexico until Europeans brought them in 1519.

We know about these ancient toys and games mainly because archaeologists (people who study the remains of past worlds) have found traces of them in graves and tombs. Egyptian tombs contain many toys, preserved by the dry desert air.

◀ **First dolls**
Deciding who made the first dolls is a tricky business. Many ancient peoples made small human figures for use in religious ceremonies, rather than as toys. Some figures may have had both uses. The Hopi people of Arizona, USA, made brightly painted *Kachina* figures like this one to use in worship, but afterwards passed them on to children.

Instead of dice, children in ancient Greece threw astragals – the square ankle bones of pigs and other animals

Organised games and sports have a very long history, too. The Olympic Games began in the ancient city of Olympia in Greece in 776 BCE. Naked athletes competed for a crown of leaves – and the glory of winning. These first Olympic Games were part of a religious festival: there was a break from the races for the sacrifice (religious killing) of 100 cattle.

Marbles ▲
More than 2,000 years ago, Roman children played the game of "nuts" by rolling hazelnuts, rounded pebbles or specially made glass balls. They weren't the first to play marbles, though. Egyptian children used clay balls for similar games many centuries before. Marbles were given their modern name when they began to be made from marble rock in the 18th century.

5

Roman Games

Armed with simple, savage weapons, two warriors enter a vast arena. The pair fight for their lives. As the loser's blood spills out on to the hot sand, 50,000 people cheer the victor! It sounds like a gory modern computer game, but it's not. To the people of Rome 2,000 years ago, deadly battles like this were popular spectator sports.

Called *munera*, the battles were part of the Roman games that also included chariot races, theatrical shows and wild animal hunts. The fighters, called gladiators, were slaves, prisoners of war or criminals. The most successful became heroes, just like today's football stars.

● ▲ **Mock naval battles**
From time to time, the arena was filled with water, and gladiators staged naval battles.

● ▼ **Matched warriors**
Gladiator combats were staged as carefully as a modern wrestling match. There were many different combinations of weapons and armour, all with special names. Here, a *retiarius* (net man) on the left fights his traditional opponent, the *secutor* (chaser).

Roman graffiti has been found that praises the gladiator Celadus as "the girls' heart-throb"

A nasty end
Combat in the Roman arena was such a terrifying experience that one gladiator chose to kill himself rather than face his foe. He slipped away to the lavatory just before his fight was due to begin, and choked himself with the filthy sponge-on-a-stick that Romans used instead of toilet paper.

Gladiators lived for the arena, and not every fight ended in death. If the loser fought well, the crowd waved handkerchiefs to signal that his life should be spared.

Fish man's helmet ▶
A gladiator's armour was matched to his risk of injury: a quick death spoiled the show! A *murmillo* (fish man) wore a strong helmet with a pierced visor to protect his face. Although this was his only armour, he also gripped a shield to protect his body. A *hoplomachus* (Greek fighter) had a helmet, a large shield and armour on one arm and leg. A *retiarius*, however, had just one arm protected by armour.

War Games

WARFARE IS DEADLY and horrible, and even the victor suffers terribly. War games, though, can be an exciting match of skills, thrills, luck and pluck. On a computer screen, war games are bloodless battles: in the past they were much more physical!

Mexico's Aztec people fought their foes in "flowery wars" dressed in feather costumes. The aim was not to kill, but the losers were later sacrificed to the sun god!

Aztec warrior ▶
The best warriors went to battle dressed in whole-body armour shaped like a jaguar or eagle. Beginners wore hardly more than a loin-cloth. This image shows a modern Mexican dressed as a warrior for the Pan American Games.

● ● ● ● ● ● ● ● ● ● ● ● ● ● ● ● ● ● ● ●

The Aztecs named their ritual battles flowery wars because feuding warriors fell like colourful petals

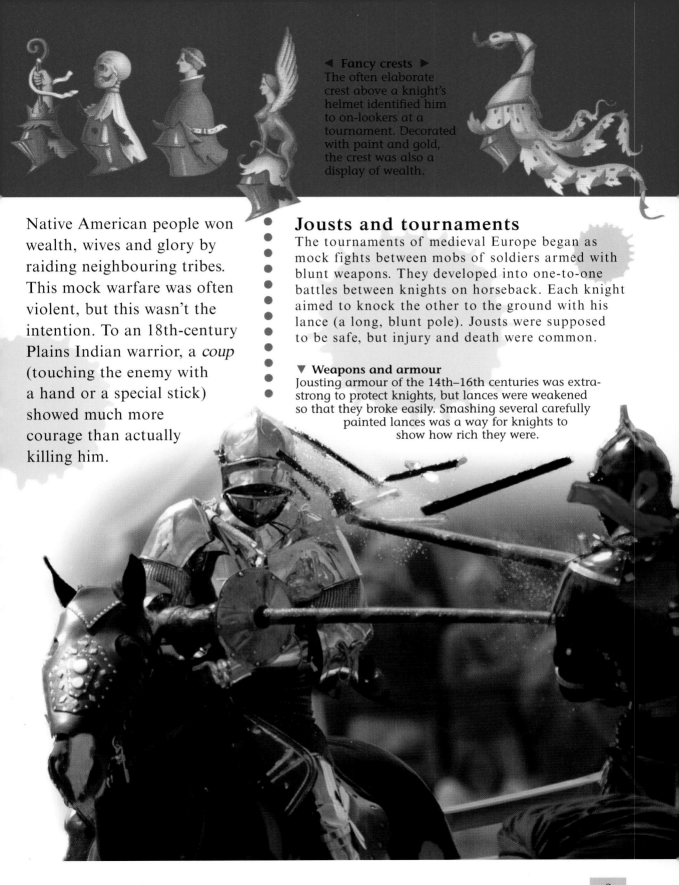

Native American people won
wealth, wives and glory by
raiding neighbouring tribes.
This mock warfare was often
violent, but this wasn't the
intention. To an 18th-century
Plains Indian warrior, a *coup*
(touching the enemy with
a hand or a special stick)
showed much more
courage than actually
killing him.

Jousts and tournaments

The tournaments of medieval Europe began as
mock fights between mobs of soldiers armed with
blunt weapons. They developed into one-to-one
battles between knights on horseback. Each knight
aimed to knock the other to the ground with his
lance (a long, blunt pole). Jousts were supposed
to be safe, but injury and death were common.

▼ Weapons and armour
Jousting armour of the 14th–16th centuries was extra-
strong to protect knights, but lances were weakened
so that they broke easily. Smashing several carefully
painted lances was a way for knights to
show how rich they were.

Pistols at Dawn

Would You Believe...?

Go for the red
Perhaps the strangest duel was fought in France in 1843. It took place between two men who had quarrelled over a game of billiards. The weapons they chose were billiard balls. The first man to throw landed the red ball on his opponent's forehead – and killed him instantly!

HOW FAR WOULD you go to settle an argument? Not long ago you might have killed the person who disagreed with you in a duel. These deadly battles were a legal way for wealthy and important people to settle rows and get revenge for insults.

Duels began as "trial by combat" 1,500 years ago. When two men both claimed something as their own, they fought to see who would keep it. People believed that God knew the true owner and would decide who won.

Duelling

Duels became a way for men who had been insulted to attempt to get their own back. The insulted man challenged his rival to a duel, and the challenged man chose the weapons they would use.

● ● ● ● ● ● ● ● ● ● ● ●

Fist fighting ▶
The modern sport of boxing began in the 19th century with bare-knuckle prize-fights. But fist fights were also popular at the ancient Olympic Games and in ancient Rome, where these figures were made some 2,100 years ago.

Modern fencing matches are safe forms of duels with swords, which were common when gentlemen wore a sword as part of their everyday clothing. Of the three types of fencing sword (foil, épée and sabre), the épée is most like the duelling sword, although its blade is made blunt to avoid injury.

▲ **Duelling pistols**
To ensure a fair fight, duelling pistols came in matched sets, like these from 1804. Duellists stood back to back (traditionally at dawn) and took an agreed number of paces before turning to fire. A "second" (friend and supporter) helped each duellist and made sure that there was no cheating.

Strict rules governed duels, but death was often the aim and this led most countries to ban it. Safer forms of combat followed. Duels turned into the fighting sports of boxing, wrestling and fencing in which both competitors live to fight again!

**The saying "pistols for two and coffee for one"
sums up the deadly end of the duel**

Eastern Arts

Taekwando students must learn a new way of thinking and a disciplined way of living

WHAT DO YOU GET when you mix warfare, athletics and philosophy (ways of thinking)? Karate, sumo, taekwando, judo and similar sports combine all these things in different ways, making Eastern martial arts very different from brutal fights and duels.

In ancient Asia, hand-to-hand fighting was a valuable survival skill. Martial arts became sports only after the invention of guns made them less important for self-defence. Westerners first learned of martial arts through 19th-century stage shows. In recent times, movies have helped to make martial arts popular ways to get fit, get happy – and even to defend yourself!

Samurai ▶
Martial arts were the trade of Japan's noble warriors, the Samurai, who fought between the 12th and 19th centuries. Shown here as a Japanese theatre character, Samurai actually fought in lightweight armour. The Samurai's main weapon was a long sword, but they also trained in unarmed fighting methods including *sumai* (see page 13) and ju-jitsu.

◀ Sumo wrestling
Twelve centuries ago, Japanese men fought to the death in bouts called *sumai*. Today's sumo wrestlers aim only to push their opponents over, or out of the ring. A fighter's weight counts for a lot, but sumo fans insist that wrestling skills are more important. Here, a grand champion shows a ritual performed before entering the ring.

Karate kid ▼
There's much more to karate than the wood-splintering "chops" for which it is famous. Meaning "empty hand" in Japanese, karate combines punching, kicking and striking with the elbow and open hand. Training also involves dance-like sequences called *kata*, which help students to remember moves.

Would You Believe...?

Heavyweights
The world's heaviest sumo wrestler, Konishiki of Hawaii, weighed 267 kg (589 lb). To keep up their weight sumo stars skip breakfast, but eat a large lunch called *chanko-nabe* washed down with beer. The wrestlers' diet and life-style is unhealthy: most die ten years younger than other Japanese people.

13

Run
for it

Speedy Greeks ▶
In the ancient Olympics,
running races were the
highlight of the games.
In the three running
events competitors raced
the length of the 200-m
stadium, ran once round
it, or completed 12 laps.

Gasping for breath, Pheidippides the messenger stumbled into Athens. Everyone was waiting for news from Marathon, where the Greeks and the Persians were at war. "We were victorious!" he gasped, then died of exhaustion. His heroic 34-km (21-mile) dash is still celebrated with the marathon running race.

Running began as a way to escape savage beasts and to carry messages. But even in Pheidippides' time, 2,500 years ago, it was already a sport as well. Today, running is among the most popular individual sports. Each year millions compete in races, or try to beat their personal best time round the block.

Super sprinter ▲
African-American sprinter Jesse Owens became an international hero at the 1936 Olympics in Berlin, Germany. He finished first in four athletics events, including the 100-m and 200-m sprints. His victory embarrassed Germany's racist rulers, the Nazis, who claimed that white people were in every way better than black people. Owens proved them wrong.

London's 1908 marathon was made 3.2 km (2 miles) longer so that it would end at the Queen's stadium seat

● ● ● ● ● ● ● ● ● ● ● ● ● ● ● ● ● ● ●

Modern marathon ▼
Each year, about 800 marathon races are held around the world. With 35,000 competitors, the New York marathon is one of the most popular. Few runners finish in less than two and a half hours, but the world record is 25 minutes less than this.

15

On the Ball

Would You Believe...?

Sorry loser
For players in the Mayan ball game *pok-a-tok*, winning was a matter of life or death – literally. Winners were as popular as today's rock stars, but losers were sometimes sacrificed (killed in a special ceremony). The Mayans perhaps believed that the sacrifice made the sun shine and the crops grow.

NO TOY IS SIMPLER than a ball – but try and count the different ways of playing with it and you will soon give up. There are many kinds of games because balls are among the most ancient of toys. Everywhere in the world, you will find a special traditional way of playing ball, with its own rules, perhaps a special ball – but always fanatical fans!

The oldest balls we know of were made in ancient Egypt 3,400 years ago. They were made of carved wood or reeds wound round and round. People everywhere made balls from whatever materials they could find. The first rubber balls came from Central America, where rubber trees grow wild.

Roman games

In the Roman ball game *harpastum*, each team of 5 to 12 players tried to keep the ball in their half of the pitch for as long as possible. Another Roman favourite, *expulsim ludere*, was a form of handball, in which players bounced the ball to each other off the wall of a special court

◄ ▲ **Volleyball, anyone?** These young ancient Roman women playing ball look remarkably modern. But the mosaic in which they appear was created 17 centuries ago in Sicily. The ball they are using is probably a small *follis*, which contained an air-filled animal bladder

The Vikings, or Norsemen, of Scandinavia (CE 800–1000) played a rough winter bat and ball game called *knattleikr* on frozen lakes and ice-covered flooded fields. Ancient Viking sagas (folk tales) describe vigorous matches that left the ice stained red with blood.

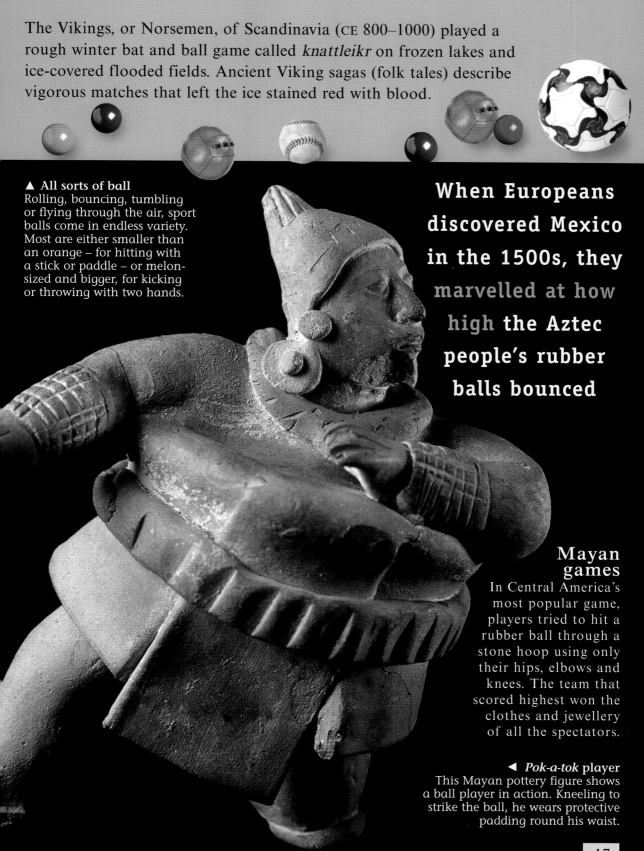

▲ All sorts of ball
Rolling, bouncing, tumbling or flying through the air, sport balls come in endless variety. Most are either smaller than an orange – for hitting with a stick or paddle – or melon-sized and bigger, for kicking or throwing with two hands.

When Europeans discovered Mexico in the 1500s, they marvelled at how high the Aztec people's rubber balls bounced

Mayan games
In Central America's most popular game, players tried to hit a rubber ball through a stone hoop using only their hips, elbows and knees. The team that scored highest won the clothes and jewellery of all the spectators.

◄ *Pok-a-tok* player
This Mayan pottery figure shows a ball player in action. Kneeling to strike the ball, he wears protective padding round his waist.

17

Rolling,
Hurling and Kicking

WITH 1,000 PLAYERS, a pitch the size of a small town and the only rule being "no killing", medieval football matches were riotous fun. These mob games pitted neighbouring villages against each other. Deaths and injuries were common, and the games flattened fields and fences and wrecked houses. No wonder England's king, Edward II, banned football in London in 1314.

▲ Calcio
In Florence, Italy, the *Calcio Storico* ball game mixes football and fighting. It began in 1530 as a way to annoy the foreign king Charles V, whose army was besieging the city.

Foul play ▶
Football has mostly shaken off its deadly past, though as this newspaper picture from 1927 shows, violent tackles continued long after mob games ended.

Football got safer in the early 19th century when schoolboys began to play the game. But each school had its own rules so when they played each other, games ended in argument. In the 1860s, agreements on standard rules for soccer – and for American football in the USA – led to the games we play today.

HEBDOMADAIRE - 38ᵉ Année
61, rue Lafayette, Paris

=ILLUSTRE=

27 Mars 1927 - N° 1892
PRIX : 50 CENTIMES

TRAGIQUE MATCH DE FOOTBALL
Même si vous n'avez pas pris part à notre Concours, ce numéro vous intéressera.

Skull ball

Thanks to its round shape, a human skull makes rather a good ball. Some balls used in the Mayan ball game *pok-a-tok* (see page 15) were made by wrapping rubber around a skull. In Britain, there is a legend that football in the town of Chester began when locals kicked around the skull of a defeated Danish prince.

Football is a devilish pastime which causes fighting, brawling, murder and great effusion of blood

Wackier ball games

Rules didn't altogether end mob football, and of course had no effect on the wilder rolling, hurling and kicking games played worldwide. Native Americans, for example, bet everything they owned on a game called *chunky*, won by hurling spears at a rolling boulder.

Deadly gridiron game ▼

Even mob football games seem safe compared to early American football. By 1905, the game had become so brutal that 18 people died on the pitch in one season. The most dangerous tackles were outlawed after US president Roosevelt threatened to ban the game unless it was made safer.

Would You Believe...? Would You Believe...? Would You Believe...?

Lunar ball game
When NASA's Apollo 14 spacecraft was launched in 1971, astronaut and golf fanatic Alan Shepard sneaked a club and two balls on board. On the Moon, he took a swing, starting the first space ball game. Aided by the Moon's low gravity, he fired one of the balls "miles and miles".

Faster than a Speeding Snail

THE CROWD ROARS AS THE RACE begins! Gamblers wave wads of money as they rush to make last-minute bets. As the racers reach the final straight, there's a disaster: a passing bird snaps up the leading runner. But when snails are racing, anything can happen!

Snail racing is just one of the newest and wackiest forms of the world's oldest entertainment. Racers drove horse-drawn chariots round Rome's vast arena 2,000 years ago, while 250,000 Romans screamed their support from the seats.

Snail's pace ▲
The internet made snail racing popular when an on-line gambling site took bets on a race in 2000.

▼ Getting the hump
Camel racing is more popular than horse racing in the Middle East. Wealthy leaders of Arab nations sponsor the sport, one of whom owns 14,000 racing camels.

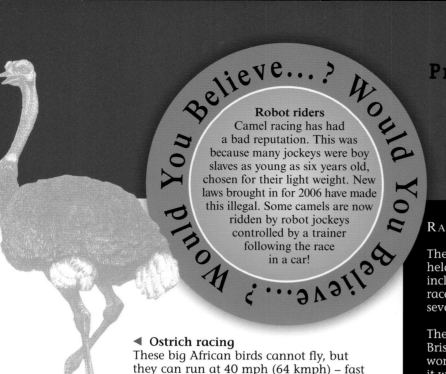

Would You Believe...?

Robot riders
Camel racing has had a bad reputation. This was because many jockeys were boy slaves as young as six years old, chosen for their light weight. New laws brought in for 2006 have made this illegal. Some camels are now ridden by robot jockeys controlled by a trainer following the race in a car!

Prized racehorses in ancient Rome lived in marble stables

◀ Ostrich racing

These big African birds cannot fly, but they can run at 40 mph (64 kmph) – fast enough to pick up a speeding fine! They are strong enough to carry an adult jockey, and racing them is a popular sport on the South African farms where they are raised.

Since ancient times, people have held every kind of race you can think of – and many more that you cannot! Racing is thrilling because nobody can be certain who will win. Betting on the result adds to the excitement, and is the only reason many races are run.

▲ Racing bacon

Once a novelty for village fêtes, pig racing became a big success in Russia in 2006. Farmers breed special racing pigs by choosing parents with long legs. Coaches and psychologists train the piglets at the Sport Pig Centre near Moscow for races on a special track later in the year.

RACING STATISTICS

The third annual **Pig** Olympics, held in Moscow, Russia, in 2006, included running races, swimming races and pig football. Pigs from seven countries took part.

The Story Bridge Hotel in Brisbane, Australia, hosts the world's oldest **cockroach** race: it was first held in 1982.

The most famous **frog** race is the Calaveras frog jumping championship held in California, USA. Two thousand frogs compete once a year to beat the 1986 record of 6.55 m (21.48 ft).

The fastest racing garden **snails** can cross the finishing line at 20 cm (8 in) a minute.

The Olympic Games featured **horse** racing for the first time in 648 BCE.

Gambling on **horse** races became such a problem in 17th-century Scotland that anyone winning more than 100 marks had to give the excess to the poor.

The annual **Ostrich** Festival is held in Chandler, Arizona, USA. Ostrich races are the main attraction – alongside stalls selling ostrich burgers and ostrich skin boots!

Beastly Pleasures

STRONG, FIERCE AND QUICK, wild animals are fascinating. Today we marvel at their survival skills in wildlife films. But in the past, animals provided stranger entertainment. The Minoan people celebrated the strength of bulls by vaulting over them. Animals in Roman times were not so lucky: they died to amuse the crowd.

In an arena in ancient Rome, gladiators fought lions and tigers. The "wild" beasts were so frightened in these brutal battles that keepers used flaming torches to drive them to fight.

▲ **Bear baiting**
Like many of her subjects, English queen Elizabeth I (1533–1603) loved to watch dogs attack a bear chained to a post. The "bait" went on until all the dogs were dead, or the bear was too wounded to fight. Specially built arenas called bear gardens showed this entertainment from the 11th century. It was banned in 1835.

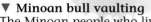

▼ **Minoan bull vaulting**
The Minoan people who lived on the Mediterranean island of Crete some 3,500 years ago worshipped bulls. Their sculptures show athletes vaulting over bulls' backs and horns. The bulls were unharmed – unlike those in Spanish *corridas* (bull fights) today.

◄ Dog fighting
Dog fighting is banned in Britain and the USA, but it continues illegally, using breeds such as the Staffordshire and Pit Bull terriers. These breeds are not just fighting dogs, though: they are also used to hunt rats, and "Staffies" make great family dogs.

Fighting the ban

The Romans eventually tired of their "hunts", but cruel animal sports have never really ended. To entertain crowds and please gamblers, animal keepers have set all sorts of beasts against each other – including ferocious dogs and roosters bred to fight to the death in the ring. Most countries ban these battles, but they still continue in secret.

Would You Believe...?

Animals in the arena
In a single Roman arena, gladiators killed up to 5,000 animals in a day. To keep up with this demand, trappers rounded up beasts in Africa and shipped them to Rome. This cruel trade grew so vast that some North African animals became extinct.

Sharp spikes **called cockspurs, up to 6.4 cm (2.5 in) long, are sometimes** attached to the birds' heels

▲ Cock fighting
Male chickens, or cockerels, are ferocious fighters even in the farmyard, using their spurs (sharp points on their legs) to wound rivals. Gamblers use the cock's fighting spirit by setting pairs in arenas called cockpits and betting on which will kill the other, as shown in this 1890s advert for a veterinary disinfectant. Cock fighting is still allowed – and popular – in many countries.

A-Hunting we shall Go

EUROPE'S RICH AND POWERFUL people set off to chase deer, pigs, badgers, foxes – and almost anything else that ran away – with a meaningless cry of "Tally-ho!". In the Middle Ages (1000–1400), hunting changed the landscape and laws. Kings and queens took the best land for themselves – punishing others who hunted there with mutilation or death.

Hunting was the only sport considered fit for members of rich, ruling families. Wealthy barons took their favourite hunting hawks to the dinner table, and even into the bedroom.

▲ Fox hunting
Like the wolves they resemble, foxes are hunted as pests because they kill farm animals. Medieval hunters called the fox a "beast of stinking flight" and chased him on horseback with dogs. Such hunts are now illegal in many countries, but foxes can still be shot as pests.

◄ Poaching
Until 1216, peasants bold – or foolish – enough to poach (hunt illegally) in royal forests faced death. The lucky ones might just have had their hands and feet cut off. Even in the 19th century, land owners caught poachers with brutal man-traps, as shown on the handle of this hunting sword.

▲ Medieval hunting
The word "forest" originally meant not woodland, but land the king claimed for hunting. In the 12th century, when this picture was drawn, royal forests covered a third of England. The animals the king hunted in the forest were fed on crops grown outside – by peasants who were forbidden to hunt them.

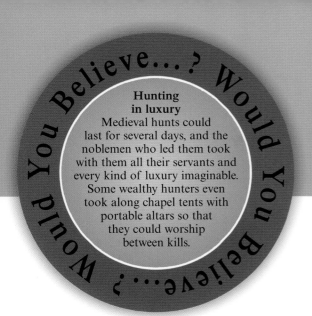

Would You Believe...? Would You Believe...? Would You Believe...?

Hunting in luxury
Medieval hunts could last for several days, and the noblemen who led them took with them all their servants and every kind of luxury imaginable. Some wealthy hunters even took along chapel tents with portable altars so that they could worship between kills.

England's King Edward III took 120 hunting hounds with him when he went to war on France

Hunting with animals

Hawks helped in hunts for small game like rabbits, but other tame animals played a big part in all hunts. Hunters could only keep up with their prey on horseback, and they relied on dogs' keen sense of smell to follow the trails of the animals and lead them in the chase. The excited barking of the pack of hounds accompanied every hunt.

Hawking ▶
Owning a hunting bird was a sign of noble status. The type of bird you owned showed how important you were. Emperors hunted with eagles or vultures, while mere knights had to make do with a kind of falcon, such as this peregrine falcon. Hawk owners hooded (blindfolded) their birds and stroked them with feathers to calm them before a hunt.

● ● ● ● ● ● ● ● ● ● ● ● ● ● ● ● ● ● ●

Traditional hunts generally ended with the death of the hunted animal, so they were called "blood sports." The obvious cruelty of hunting has led to campaigns to stop it. In countries where hunting is now banned, hunters still enjoy the thrill of the chase – without harming any animals. They set their hounds to follow a trail laid by dragging a strong-smelling object.

25

Circus and Fairground

S HOWMAN PHINEAS T. BARNUM loaded his vast circus on to a railway train for its 1872 American tour, boasting that it was "The Greatest Show on Earth". He was probably right: it took 65 trucks to carry the tent, rings, animals and performers.

Barnum did not invent the circus, though. Englishman Phillip Astley first filled a ring with sawdust in 1768. He made it 13 m (42 ft) wide because he knew he could stand upright on the back of a horse cantering round a circle just this big.

▲ **Acrobatics**
Tricks on horseback amused early circus audiences, along with tightrope and trapeze acts. Frenchman Jules Léotard introduced the first circus trapeze act in 1859.

◄ **Animal acts**
Circus audiences once expected to watch lions "tamed" in the ring, and see other beasts perform tricks, like this boxing kangaroo. Cruelty concerns put an end to most animal acts.

Would You Believe...?

Famous farter
French baker Joseph Pujol usually performed on stage, but his strange act was perfectly suited to the circus. From 1887–1914, he entertained audiences as *Le Pétomane* (the fartist). His long, odourless farts imitated animals, musical instruments, canons, thunder and even earthquakes.

The golden age of circus

By 1825, circuses had a winning combination. Under a "big top" (tent), they staged strange and wonderful acts and showed off exotic animals, while the surrounding fairground dazzled visitors. The golden age of circus lasted until the early 20th century.

Clowning around ▶
Clowns make fun of people and help us to see the silly side of things we all do. They developed from the 16th-century Italian *Commedia dell'Arte* (artists' comedy), in which characters wore masks. English clown Joseph Grimaldi started the tradition of white-faced clowning in the early 1800s.

Amazing feats

Anyone special could make a living in the circus (or outside it). The weirder the act, the more the public would pay. Phineas Barnum said of his customers, "There's a sucker born every minute."

• In 1860, Barnum showed the original "Siamese twins" Chang and Eng, who were joined at the chest. Both were married, and they had 22 children between them.
• Kar-mi's act was to swallow an electric light, which could be seen glowing inside him.
• The original Tom Thumb was 71 cm (28 in) high at the age of 22.
• The greatest high-wire artist of all was Blondin (Jean-Francois Gravelet, 1824–1897). His most famous act was to cross the Niagara Falls on a tightrope in 1859.

▲ Ringling Brothers

The American Ringling family started a circus in 1884, but they were not successful until they bought an elephant four years later. By 1907, the Ringling Brothers had bought Barnum's famous circus and were the biggest show in the USA, with a tent seating 10,000 people.

Even today, clowns are nicknamed "Joey" in honour of Joseph Grimaldi

Defying Gravity

A SLOW, NERVOUS CLIMB; a moment of sheer terror at the top; then the wonderful, terrifying zoom downwards. Nothing beats the thrill of a white-knuckle ride! A winch lifts the cars up the first hill, but it is gravity that drives the rest of the swooping journey.

White-knuckle rides began as winter ice-slides in 16th-century Russia. One of the first with wheeled cars started as a mine railway, built in 1827 in Pennsylvania, USA. Passengers soon replaced coal in the trucks on the Mauch Chunk Gravity Railroad, screaming in terror as they rode the 29-km (18-mile) track.

Roller coasters

In 1884, the first real roller coaster opened at Coney Island in New York. Cars travelled only at running speed but, before long, ride designers were building mountainous wooden tracks to make rides faster – and scarier.

Would You Believe...?

Feel the force
The world's fastest roller coasters push riders down into their seats with a maximum force of 4 g (four times the force of gravity). This is a third greater than the g-force astronauts feel during the launch of NASA's Space Shuttle. It is possible to build even faster rides, but passengers would lose consciousness.

◀ **Ice-slide**
Bored Russians in the 18th century amused themselves by plunging down wooden slides like this one. The "cars" were blocks of ice fitted with wooden seats. Russian empress Catherine the Great was a fan, sliding screaming with delight down the steep slopes.

COOPER STREET. MANCHESTER.

▲ **Centrifugal railway**
Russian ice-slides inspired small, wheeled
indoor rides like this "Centrifugal Railway",
built in an old theatre in the 1850s in
Manchester, England. Riders sitting in small
carts whirled through two loops on their
way from the balcony to the stage.

Steel rides ▶
The tight turns and
enormous speed of
rides today are possible
because they are made
from steel. Karl
Bacon designed
the first steel
tube roller coaster,
Matterhorn Bobsleds,
which opened in
Disneyland in 1959.

Water Sports

Scuba diving ▶
Diving for pleasure really began when Frenchmen Jacques Cousteau and Émile Gagnan invented Scuba (Self-Contained Underwater Breathing Apparatus) in 1942. Previously, divers breathed air pumped from the surface of the water down a tube.

OCEANS COVER TWO-THIRDS OF EARTH'S surface. We live on a wet planet, yet most of us have never spent more than a few moments under water. Those who have, however, do not seem to want to get out of the waves. They wriggle into rubber wet suits and strap on scuba kit – tanks of air that let them swim as free as fishes for about 40 minutes at a time.

Scuba diving is one of the world's fastest-growing sports, but this is just one way to have fun in the wet. There are weirder and wackier water sports, such as free diving, extreme surfing and waterfall plunges. In most of them, the thrill comes from the danger: the risk of drowning is never far away.

▼ Bog snorkelling
Fancy swimming through a chilly peat bog? Amazingly, hundreds of people do. The world bog snorkelling championship takes place each summer at Llanwrtyd Wells in Wales.

The most daring free divers grip a heavy sledge that drags them quickly into deep water

Cave divers plunge into flooded caverns and tunnels. If anything goes wrong, they cannot just swim to the surface. Free divers don't bother with scuba: they hold their breath to swim down as deep as 120 m (390 ft).

▲ **Deep sea pioneer**
Macedonian king Alexander the Great was among the first to enjoy a spell under water. According to legend, he was lowered into the sea in a barrel in 332 BCE. When he came up for air, he declared "The world is lost. The big fish eat the little ones."

Would You Believe...? Would You Believe...?

Niagara Falls
In 1901, 63-year-old school teacher Annie Taylor climbed into a barrel and rolled over Niagara Falls on the USA/Canada border. Climbing out at the bottom, she said "No-one ought ever do that again," but she started an unofficial sport that has since killed a third of those who try it.

▲ **Extreme surfing**
For the ultimate big-wave thrill, surfers hitch a tow out to sea from a helicopter or jet-ski. This enables them to ride waves bigger and faster than any they could paddle out to. Called tow-in surfing, it is not for the timid. Falling from these huge breakers can crush surfers on rocks, or hold them under water for up to a minute.

Taking the Air

First flight ▶
German Otto Lilienthal launched his bat-wing gliders from a home-made hill. After more than 200 safe flights, a gust of wind upset his craft in 1896 and he fell to his death.

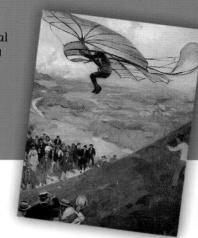

SOARING HIGH ABOVE THE ground like a bird is a dream that has always enchanted people. In ancient Greek myths, Daedalus and his son Icarus made wings from wax and feathers. Icarus crashed when he flew too close to the Sun and melted the wax. For centuries, most would-be bird-men were no more successful.

In the 11th century, a jump from a tower killed an English monk called Eilmer. Otto Lilienthal, inventor of the hang-glider, died when one of his craft crashed. Wilbur and Orville Wright made flight safer when they perfected a flying machine in 1905.

The chance that a plane might crash during a daring stunt drew crowds to air shows

Barnstormers ▶
Would-be American flyers bought cheap surplus planes when World War I ended in 1918. Nicknamed barnstormers, they flew reckless stunts like wing-walking at small-town aviation shows.

Flying soon became a popular sport. Aircraft were little more than box-kites with engines, and anyone with enough skill – and money – could build one. Rich and famous people bought planes and raced them, or flew them for pleasure.

Thrill-seekers

Today, anyone can take to the sky after a few hang-glider lessons, but simple flight is too tame for some. Serious thrill-seekers parachute from towers or bridges, or plunge from aircraft on surf boards.

Hang-gliding ▲
Like Lilienthal, today's hang-glider pilots control their fragile, kite-like craft by shifting their weight around in the harness that hangs from the rigid-framed wing.

BASE jumping ▶
You do not necessarily need an aircraft to use a parachute. BASE jumpers leap from places nearer the ground. BASE stands for the high spots the jumpers use: Buildings, Antennae, Spans (such as bridges) and Earth (cliffs). Because these launch points are relatively low, there is not very much time for the parachute to open, and the sport is highly dangerous.

33

Land
Daredevils

YOU DO NOT NEED to get soaking wet or strap on wings to risk your life for pleasure. Land sports offer plenty of dangerous thrills. Most involve the risk of rock and human flesh meeting at great speed. Bungee jumping, for instance, relies on nothing but a strip of elastic to keep the two apart.

Modern bungee jumping looks risky, but is nothing like as dangerous as the Pacific Island pastime from which it grew. Modern mountaineering also looks very different from when it began in the late 18th century. Then, climbers wore only tweed suits for warmth and knotted hemp ropes round their waists for safety.

◀ **Bungee jump**
The land divers of Pentecost Island in the South Pacific plunge from special towers, with vines tied to their ankles. The vines stop them just as their heads touch the ground – which is carefully dug over to provide a softer landing if a vine snaps.

The world's highest bungee jump is 216 m (708 ft) tall – the height of a 52-storey building

◀ Rock climbing

When climbers had reached the summits of all the world's great peaks, they looked for harder ways to get to the top. From the 1960s, they scaled vertical cliffs with the help of metal spikes (pitons) hammered into the rock.

Today, specialised equipment and high-performance clothing protects climbers. They still find ways to risk their lives in search of thrills, however, tackling crags and cliffs that early climbers would have thought impossible.

▶ Vertical dancing

Free climbing uses ropes only for protection against falls, not to help climbers get up the rock. The most daring and skilled form of free climbing is free soloing, in which climbers ascend alone and without ropes to catch them. They dare not place a foot wrong.

Nice Ice

◄ **Speed skating**
Wearing clingy outfits and streamlined helmets to reduce their air resistance, speed skaters circle their icy tracks at a frightening 45 kmph (28 mph).

FROZEN WATER WILL turn any surface into a slide and make difficult tasks – like mountaineering – even more of a challenge. Many of today's winter sports began for sensible reasons: skating, for example, allowed people to cross frozen rivers from 1,000 BCE. Now these pastimes offer excitement that is hard to match in any other sport.

Skaters enjoy their sport on perfectly flat and level ice; climbers are the only ones who aim to "up" the ice; all other winter sports use the formula "gravity plus ice equals speed". They career downhill, and the faster the better.

◄ **Ice climbing**
A frosty coating makes rock slippery, but it can also make impossible surfaces – like waterfalls – climbable. Ice climbers use boot spikes called crampons and specially shaped axes to get a grip.

▲ **Ice skating**
The people of Scandinavia were probably the first to go ice skating, using bone or antler skates to skid wildly across frozen rivers. These English bone skates are about 800 years old. Faster ice skates with metal blades were probably a Dutch invention of the 17th century.

The slopes that steep skiers ride are so extreme that snow barely sticks to them

36

Speed skiing is the fastest sport without a motor: experts reach 240 kmph (150 mph). They move so fast that their skis don't even touch the snow, and a fall causes burns as well as broken bones.

▼ **Bobsleighing**
Bobsleighs are a sleeker, faster hi-tech version of the sledge. They hurtle down specially built ice tracks as fast as speeding cars. On the corners, the crews are pressed sideways at 5 g (five times the force of gravity).

Would You Believe...? Would You Believe...? Would You Believe...?

Exploration – or sport?
When polar exploration began in about 1910, heroic adventurers risked their lives racing to the frozen tips of the planet. Today, anyone with $67,000 and 11 weeks to spare can ski across Antarctica to the South Pole. (The Arctic is more tricky – it's melting!)

Flying and sliding

Ski-fliers launch themselves from purpose-built ramps in an extreme form of ski-jumping. The best ski-fliers travel nearly 240 m (800 ft) – the length of 28 buses parked nose to tail. At least a bobsleigh offers some protection. Bobsleigh races began in 1884 in Switzerland, and the first narrow, terrifying courses were built 20 years later.

Feats of Endurance

EATING INSECTS, running long distances, walking on fire: challenges like these are gruelling, painful and even downright dangerous. So why are they growing in popularity? Often people take part to prove that they can overcome fear and disgust, or put up with pain and hardship.

In Europe, these difficult tasks perhaps began in the Middle Ages with ordeals. Then, people accused of crimes did them to prove that they were innocent. Elsewhere, ordeals tested those joining secret societies and other special groups.

Locust

▲ **Bush tucker challenge**
Yucky TV food ordeals, such as eating dishes of caterpillars, are not all they seem. Many kinds of insect are edible, wholesome food and contain as much protein as best steak. Insects make up an important part of the diet in some country areas of Asia and Africa.

Games and shows
Today there's money and fame to be had in feats of endurance. Ordinary people can get on TV if they are willing to endure discomfort at best, and deadly danger at worst. And television audiences will tune in for a chance to watch celebrities doing something that they find gross or humiliating.

▲ **Fire-walking**
In many different societies around the world, people used to prove their religious faith or superhuman powers by walking on hot coals. Today, fire-walking is a popular way to overcome fear. It is safe if feet and coals are correctly prepared, but some walkers still burn their feet so never try this yourself!

▼ Trial by ordeal
Some medieval ordeal defendants had to carry red-hot metal bars. The "trial by accursed morsel" may have been easier: the challenge was to eat a feather sandwich.

People in the Middle Ages believed that ordeals would not harm those who had done no wrong

▲ Endurance festival
In Japanese universities, students have traditionally challenged each other to *Gaman Taikai* (tough-it-out) contests. A TV programme in the 1980s called *Za Gaman* made the contests famous outside Japan. It set the style for today's reality-show TV ordeals. The games are still popular in Japan – in this one, men and women strip and splash ice-cold water on themselves.

Shall we Dance?

A MUSICAL BEAT IS HARD TO resist: you just have to get on your feet and dance. Though we do it mainly for pleasure today, traditional dances are also part of ancient rituals and religion. And indeed, this is probably how dance began.

▲ **Ball-gown elegance**
This English couple from 1680 are dancing in the style that had recently become popular. The woman is hitching up her dress to show off her steps.

In Stone-Age Europe, shamans (tribal sorcerers) may have been trying to bring hunters good luck by dressing in animal skins. Their dancing steps imitated the beasts the hunters were seeking. Later dances were a form of worship.

The Italian dance *the tarantella* **began as a frantic cure for a spider bite**

◄ **Whirling Dervishes**
Spinning like a top is a form of worship for Dervishes – members of a Turkish Muslim group called the Sufis. The Dervishes believe their whirling around brings them closer to Allah (God).

Plague dance
A dance frenzy spread across medieval Europe just as a plague called the Black Death was killing a third of the population. Dancers screamed, foamed at the mouth and made leaping steps. The cause may have been panic – or ergot, a mood-altering chemical found in mouldy grain.

◀ **Sri Lankan devil dance**
To help cure madness, illness or bad luck, Sri Lanka's devil dancers leap through the air and whirl flames. They aim to banish demons from their patients. Though the dancers are men, their costumes make them look half female.

In a 1930s dance marathon in Chicago, USA, the winners danced for seven months

Dirty dancing
Because it brings men and women close together, dancing has always had a rude reputation. In England, mixed dancing was labelled sinful and ungodly in the 17th century. A hundred years later, the waltz was thought too rude in some places – though it is now utterly respectable.

Elvis the Pelvis ▶
The hip-swinging dance movements of singer Elvis Presley (1935–1977) earned him the nickname "the Pelvis". Presley's sexy shaking was too much for 1950s television audiences. When he appeared on a popular show, cameras filmed him only from the waist up.

• • • • • • • • • • • • • • • • • •

Dancing has a darker past, too. When diseases killed millions in Europe, dancing mania was just as infectious, making people dance hysterically. In the 1920s and 30s in the USA, dance marathons kept out-of-work couples dancing day and night. The last couple to drop won a cash prize.

41

Helping the Year Go Round

CHRISTMAS AND EASTER, Diwali and Passover all add annual excitement to the calendar, but they are not the only events that help the year go round. Every day there's a festival going on somewhere. Tiny, weird and wacky, some are hardly known outside the village that celebrates them. But others are major national holidays.

Would You Believe...? Would You Believe...?

Too many saints?
Each year, Catholics celebrate saints' days. However, there are so many saints that a devout Catholic could be celebrating every day – several times! No saint has a day all of their own. Things get especially busy on February 5th, when no fewer than 23 saints enjoy a festival.

◄ **Shrove Tuesday**
Shrove Tuesday is the day before a Christian fast (a time when religious people give up certain foods). Christians were not supposed to eat butter or eggs during the Fast of Lent, so they used these up in pancakes or other pastries.

Britain has some of the smallest and quaintest celebrations, often with strict rules and odd costumes. Many of the ceremonies and processions keep alive ancient rights granted to villages by their rulers centuries ago. But nobody knows how many others started.

The Burryman of Queensferry ►
On a summer's day each year, a strange figure tours this Scottish town, collecting money in silence. He is covered in the seed pods of the burr thistle and has a rose crown. Townspeople believe that bad luck will follow if the Burryman stops making his annual tour.

Short for "All Hallow's Eve", Halloween is the day before the Christian festival of All Hallows (holy) Day on 1 November. But before Christianity reached Britain, 1 November was the Day of the Dead for Britain's Celtic people, who left out food for their ancestors' ghosts to eat.

Religion provides a reason for huge numbers of annual events. The more religions, the more festivals there are. India – where people follow Islam, Hinduism, Buddhism, Christianity, Jainism or one of many other smaller religions – probably has more annual holidays than any other country.

Pagans and Christians

Before Christianity became Europe's main religion, everyone celebrated the passing seasons with festivals. To stop these pagan (non-Christian) ceremonies, Christians scheduled festivals for the same days. Many of today's festivals have pagan roots.

Scary masks remind us that Halloween was thought to be the day the dead came to life

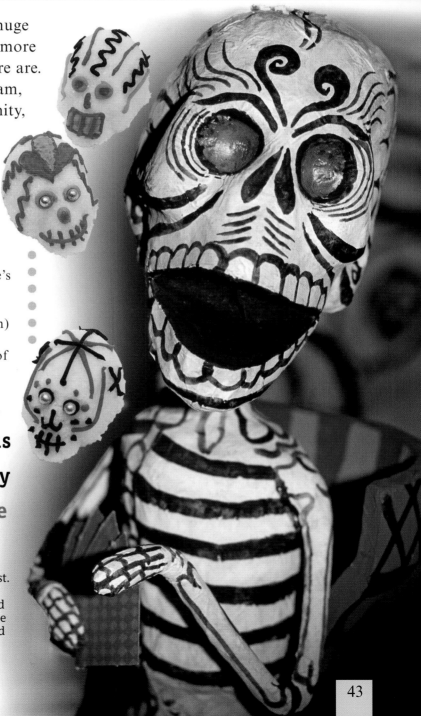

Day of the Dead ▶
Mexicans honour their ancestors with a joyful festival held around November 1st. Called the *Dia de Muertos* (Day of the Dead), it's a chance to visit graves, build small household shrines – and exchange grisly presents in the shape of skulls and skeletons. Many gifts are edible: bread and sugar treats are especially popular.

43

What's so Weird about That?

AS TIMES HAVE CHANGED, sports and games have changed – though sometimes less than you might expect. Gladiators no longer fight to the death, but you can still watch boxers beat each other senseless. The cruellest animal sports – such as bear baiting – are banned, but hunting and fishing are still popular.

So what's weird, and what's not? Things that seem normal now – such as music and dancing – were once outlawed. And to people from the past, today's extreme sports might seem pointlessly risky.

Would You Believe…? Would You Believe…?

A harmless round of golf?
Games and sports are not always as harmless as they seem. Golf doesn't have the bloody reputation of gladiator combat, but courses can ruin the environment. An 18-hole course uses as much water as a town of 10,000 people, and can turn the surrounding land to desert.

◄ **Nothing new**
Spinning in a circular cage – a space ball – is one of the latest fairground thrills. But nothing is ever really new in leisure: it is just re-invented. These roller wheels from 1927 are just like modern-day space balls.

How odd is your favourite pastime?
Compared to the way you spend your free time, some of the pastimes in this book may seem very odd. But as long as what we do for leisure and pleasure doesn't harm others, does it really matter if it's weird and wacky – or just plain daft?

"Old-fashioned" pastimes have a habit of reappearing with new names

Find out More

You can find out lots more about surprising leisure activities from these websites and places to visit.

Websites

Toys and games
http://www.historychannel.com/exhibits/
toys/index.html
Find out how some of your favourite toys and games started on this interactive History Channel site.

Gladiators
http://www.bbc.co.uk/history/ancient/romans/
launch_gms_gladiator.shtml#
This BBC website challenges you to equip a virtual gladiator with the correct weapons and armour, and push him into a virtual arena to meet his fate.

Jousting
http://www.tudorbritain.org/joust/
A medieval battle game that lets you relive the thrills and spills of the tournament.

Find a clown
http://www.annualclownsdirectory.com/
Need a circus clown in a hurry? You can find one on this directory of British clowns.

Roller coaster
http://virtual.questacon.edu.au/Roller coaster/
The ultimate white-knuckle website: build a virtual roller coaster from a kit of parts, then race around it in a dizzying ride!

Ball games
http://www.ballgame.org
A spectacular interactive website about the famous ball game of Central America: find out what the players wore, learn the rules, then play the game.

Feats of endurance
http://news.nationalgeographic.com/kids/2004/04/
eatingbugs.html
Check out this site for recipes that will make your lunch box creep and crawl.

Places to visit

The Circus Space
Coronet Street
London
N1 6HD
Telephone: 020 7613 4141
Website: http://www.thecircusspace.co.uk
Whether you want to juggle, fly on a trapeze or ride a unicycle, you can learn to do it at Circus Space, Britain's top circus skills school.

National football museum
Sir Tom Finney Way
Deepdale
Preston
PR1 6RU
Telephone: 01772 908 442
Website: http://www.nationalfootballmuseum.com/
This museum tells the story of football from the earliest times to the present day. There are exhibits about famous teams and players – and you can appear on a special edition of a TV football show with Gary Lineker.

Learn to scuba dive
Website: http://www.bsac.com/meet/
meetbranch.html
If you want to be a Scuba diver, check out the British Sub Aqua Club website to find a local pool where you can learn in complete safety.

Jousting
Website: http://www.knightsroyal.co.uk/
To hear splintering lances and crashing armour, visit a jousting spectacular. The Knights of Royal England put on displays from April to September.

Toy museum
V&A Museum of Childhood
Cambridge Heath Road
London
E2 9PA
Telephone: 020 8983 5200
Website: http://www.vam.ac.uk/moc/index.html
This museum has displays of children's clothes from the past as well as toys, games, dolls, doll houses and teddy bears.

Glossary

Did you read anything you didn't understand? Some of the more complicated and unusual terms used in this book are explained here.

armour
Protective clothing often made of metal, worn in battle to prevent injuries.

Aztecs
People who ruled Mexico before it was conquered by Spanish explorers in the 16th century.

barnstormer
Skilled aircraft pilot who performs flying tricks for a living.

blood sport
Sport that involves killing animals.

boxing
Fist fight, now usually with padded gloves.

bungee jumping
Sport of jumping from high points with an elastic rope fixed to the legs to break the fall.

bush tucker
Food gathered from the wild, especially grubs.

devil
An evil god.

Diwali
"Festival of Lights" celebrated by followers of the Hindu religion in October or November.

extinct
No longer living anywhere on Earth.

gamble
A deal (called a bet) made with another person about an unpredictable event, in which the one who correctly guesses the result wins money from the other.

glider
Aircraft that soars through the air without an engine.

gravity
Natural force that pulls together heavy objects. Gravity is the force that makes things fall downwards on Earth.

joust
Competition between mounted knights using long pole-like weapons called lances to knock each other from their horses.

Maya
People who ruled Central America and part of Mexico until Spanish conquest in the 16th century.

Minoans
People who lived on the Greek island of Crete for more than 1,000 years from about 2,600 BCE.

mosaic
Picture made up of hundreds of tiny pieces of coloured pottery or stone.

NASA
The National Aeronautics and Space Administration – the USA's space agency.

Nazi
Political party that ruled Germany (1933–1945) under the control of its leader Adolf Hitler.

Olympic Games
International sports contest held every four years, in imitation of a similar event in ancient Greece.

parachute
Large fabric wing or pocket worn when jumping from a great height, which fills with air to slow the descent.

Passover
Spring festival in which Jews celebrate their ancestors' escape from Egypt.

racism
The mistaken belief that people of one race or skin colour are better than another.

shaman
Non-Christian priest believed to possess powers, such as the ability to foretell the future, cure illness or control the weather.

shrine
Small place of worship, often found in a home.

Siamese twins
Twins born joined together.

Viking
Scandinavian people who sailed as pirates from CE 800–1,050.

waltz
Dance in which men and women perform matching steps with their bodies held close together.

Index

Picture credits

The publisher would like to thank the following for their kind permission to reproduce their photographs:

Position key: c=centre; b=bottom; l=left; r=right; t=top

Cover: Front: tr: Getty Images/Steve Fitchett; cr: Getty Images/George Marks; bl: Visual&Written SL/Alamy; tl: RubberBall/Alamy. Back: OUP/Photodisc.

1: The Art Archive/Archaeological Museum Copan Honduras/Dagli Orti; 4c: George H H Huey/Corbis; 4cr: Sawyers Photographic; 5cr: Sawyers Photographic; 5t The British Museum/Heritage Images; 6b: Ann Ronan Picture Library/Heritage; 7c: The British Museum/Heritage Images; 8br: Reuters/Corbis; 9b: David Cheskins/Pa/Empics; 10br: The British Museum/Heritage Images; 11c: The Board of Trustess of the Armouries/Heritage Images; 12r: Asaian Art 7 Archaeology, inc/Corbis; 13tr: Reuters/Corbis; 13c: Franco Vogt/Corbis; 14cl: Hulton-Deutsch/Corbis; 15b: Mary Altaffer/Ap/Empics; 16bl: The Art Archive/Dagli Orti; 16cr: The Art Archive/Dagli Orti; 17c: Akg-Images/Francois Guenet; 18tl: The Art Archive/Domencia Del Corriere/Dagli Orti; 18br: The Bridgeman Art Library; 19br: Bettmann/Corbis; 20b: Craig Lovell/Corbis; 20tr: Sawyers Photographic; 21cl: Reuters/Corbis; 22tr: The British Library/Heritage Images; 22b: The British Museum/Heritage Images; 23c: Swim Ink 2, llc/Corbis; 23tl: Sawyers Photographic; 23tc: Sawyers Photographic; 24bl: Ann Ronan Picture Library/Heritage; 24bc: The Board of Trustes of the Armouries/Heritage Images; 25r: Staffan Widstrand/Corbis; 27tl: Corbis; 27cr: The National Archives/Heritage Images; 28bl: Historical Picture Archives/Corbis; 29c: Rui Vieira/Pa/Empics; 29tr: Science Museum Pictorial; 30b: Benjamin Stansall/Epa/Corbis; 31cr: Rick Doyle/Corbis; 31tl: The British Library/Heritage Images; 32b: Bettmann/Corbis; 32tr: Oxford Science Archive/Heritage Images; 33r: Shamshahrin Shamsudin/Epa/Corbis; 34l: Anders Ryman/Corbis; 35c: Stefan Schuetz/Zefa/Corbis; 36l: Sportschrome/Empics; 36cr: Museum of London/Heritage Images; 37c: Matthias Rietschel/Ap/Empics; 38bl: Stapleton Collection/Corbis; 39c: Issei Kato/Reuters/Corbis; 39tl: Sawyers Photographic; 40bl: Archivo Iconographico, S.A./Corbis; 41r: Bettmann/Corbis; 42br: Homer Sykes/Alamy; 42cl: Sawyers Photographic; 43r: J Marshall-Tribaleye Images/Alamy; 43 c: Sawyers Photographic; 44bl: Mary Evans Picture Library